Taking Breath

A play

Sarah Daniels

Samuel French—London
New York-Toronto-Hollywood

Please see page iv for further copyright information.

TAKING BREATH

Presented as part of the BT National Connections scheme at the Cottesloe Theatre, Royal National Theatre on 9th July 1999 by the Hall Green Little Theatre Youth Section, Birmingham, with the following cast:

Alana	Laura Bucknall
Gemma	Gemma Clynn
Elliot	James Weetman
Steve	Ben McLaughlin
Rachel	Julie King
Lucy	Jenny Ash
Jamie	Jessica Close
Cassie	Corinne Macaulay
Tom	Alex Harding
Kelly	Laura Kate Howcroft
The Man	Andy Holmes

Directed by Holly Taylor and Roy Palmer
Head of Sound, Kate Lyons
Sound Operating Assistant, Christopher Moody
Head of Lighting, Holly Taylor
Lighting Operator Assistant, Charlie Mulira
Stage Manager, Oliver Scott
Costume, Laura Bucknall, Corinne Macaulay and Jean Wilde
Set Building, Neil Bucknall and Bill Bucknall
Technical Assistance, Mike Nicholas

CHARACTERS

Alana, sixteen
Gemma, Alana's sister; fourteen
Elliot, seventeen
Steve, Elliot's step-brother; twenty
Rachel, Elliot's sister; nineteen
Lucy, fifteen
Jamie, sixteen
Cassie, seventeen
Tom, nineteen
Kelly, eighteen
Man, voice only

TAKING BREATH

A living-room

When the Lights come up Alana is staring at a TV. The sound of the TV is switched off. Beside her is the remote control

Gemma enters carrying an old biscuit tin

Alana What do you want?
Gemma Nothing.
Alana Piss off then.
Gemma Turn the sound up.

Alana grabs the remote but does not turn the sound up

Alana It's the news.
Gemma Yeah.
Alana You must have such a sad life.
Gemma Don't you think it's appropriate to be sad today? She was your great-grandmother as well.
Alana Appropriate? What sort of word is that, for someone your age? Who do you think you are? You don't even wear a bra.
Gemma At least I made the effort to go to her funeral.
Alana I'm grounded, remember?
Gemma Not in the daytime.
Alana (*about the biscuit tin*) What's that?
Gemma It's some of her stuff, from the home. Mum and Dad thought it might be appropriate to my history course work.

Alana They gave it to you? What about Nanna?

Gemma Grandma didn't want it. She thought I'd appreciate it.

Alana Did she say anything about me not being there?

Gemma Only that perhaps it was for the best, in the circumstances. (*About the TV*) Please turn it up.

Alana What for?

Gemma (*about the TV*) Quick. Please. It's that road protest.

Alana All those dirty hippies. Who cares. Someone should tell them if we had more roads then there'd be less asthmatics.

Gemma If I was you I'd go down there and point that out to them then!

Alana Yeah, really. What is their problem? So trees get cut down, so? Others get planted all the time but if a person stops breathing then you can't do nothing. (*Realizing what she has said*) No-one can ...

Beat

Gemma Go on, turn it up. I want to hear it because Great-Grandma once worked in one of those houses they want to pull down, you know ...

Alana Just shut up. You don't know that.

Gemma She told me.

Alana She was so Harpic she never knew what she was saying.

Gemma She told me she was in service.

Alana In the war you mean?

Gemma Not the armed services, you idiot. Like a live-in maid.

Alana Don't go writing about that in your stupid history assignment. We don't want all those stuck-up arses in that bloody boffin snob school to think we're descended from servants.

Gemma She was also one of the first women to go to university even though they weren't allowed to ——

Alana Yawn, yawn. I'm sure they didn't mean you to write about her. She's only just died.

Gemma History is not only the last millennium. It's last week, it's yesterday — it's the second just gone — from when I walked in here till now is history.

Alana I wish it was. What's the point of it though? Doing a moronic little project.

Gemma So I don't end up like you.

Alana throws the remote at her. It misses

(*Picking it up*) Thank you. (*She points the remote towards the TV*)

Alana (*as if seeing a photo of Elliot on the TV*) Go on then. Turn it up.

Gemma I'm trying ...

Alana You can say that again.

Gemma It's not working now.

Alana Look at him. Come on.

Gemma I can't. I think I've broken it. Who?

Alana Him. That tree protester bloke. (*She makes a teeth kissing noise*) He's well fit.

Gemma That's just what he isn't. He's been in a coma for a week.

Alana Oh. Has he?

Gemma Yep.

Alana How come?

Gemma Maybe at your age you should stop wasting all your time thinking about yourself and start watching the news.

Alana Give us the remote then ...

Gemma No. Fuck off.

Alana What? Right, that's it. I'm telling Mum you said that.

Gemma And who do you think she'll believe? (*Making sure she can get away*) After what you've done, she'll never trust you again. Loser.

Gemma leaves quickly, fearing Alana's reaction

Alana merely stares ahead at the silent TV

SCENE 2

A special care room in a hospital

*Steve and Rachel sit at Elliot's bedside. They look very upset but
remain completely frozen in their positions*

Elliot suddenly sits up. Steve and Rachel remain as statues

Elliot   Would you look at them? Look how upset they are. This is
revenge I've only ever been able to fantasize about. They're sorry
now. Yes! Even him. Look at him. He's always hated me and now
he's paying for it. The times he's threatened to kill me. Ha, ha.
He's my step-brother. Thank God. If I'd had his genes in me, I'd
have killed myself. And her, my big sister, Rachel. She's just like
a cat. You know how evil they are, swiping at a bird or mouse,
maiming it, then playing around with it for the sheer pleasure of
being spiteful? Well, they most probably learnt how to do that
from her. Let me give you a for instance. The first time I brought
a girl to the house who, by the way, Rachel insisted on referring
to as "Elliot's babe". Like if girls are sexist it doesn't count or
what? Anyway, I was wary because she was being a bit too curly-
lipped-OK-friendly. Then she produces it. When I was eight
Mum used to be an agent for Kays Catalogue. I once drew over
the underwear pages, crudely embellishing the photos of the
models with the help of a felt tip pen by sketching in the rude bits
that the underwear was covering. And, unknown to me, my sister,
the sadistic pervert, had kept it for all those years waiting for the
perfect moment to expose me, if you'll pardon the expression.
She didn't actually show it to the girl or anything but the threat was
there all evening. I hope she remembers that now and every other
humiliating little thing she's done and I hope she's sorry she's
thinking suicidally. At least she and me have the same dad. Did
have. He died of lung cancer when I was two. (*About Steve*) But
him. His mum just got pissed off and went. And I know, I know
kids aren't meant to be blamed for that but there's got to be

exceptions to every rule and he's one of them. His dad shacked up with Mum and then buggered off leaving him with her. She could hardly chuck him out. He's twenty now and the only job he could get was as a scab. The only thing he seems able to cook for himself is toast with brown sauce on. He can't seem to get the hang of any of the basics in life, like white things should be washed separately in the machine. Mum still has to do his ironing. Where is she, though? She should be here, shouldn't she, at my bedside? Mum? Oh no. Now, I remember. She's away. I hope they haven't dragged her back. It's the first time she's been away without us. Maybe it's me. Maybe I've been away years. No, I can't have. Those two look exactly the same. This is now. I am Elliot. I am here. I am here, now. How did I get here? Where was I to get here now? Try to remember Elliot. (*He shuts his eyes*)

SCENE 3

A tree platform. A week earlier. Night

Jamie, Cassie, Tom and Kelly are on a platform in a tree. Cassie has an unlit torch. Tom has a rope in his hand. There are five sets of handcuffs

Jamie Right?

Tom makes sure that the rope is secure

Tom Yeah, great. You?

Cassie switches her torch on

Cassie Everyone got a torch?
Jamie I've got a couple of candles and a box of matches in my pocket ——
Kelly (*groaning*) Jamie ...
Cassie Good thinking. We're stuck up a tree. One gust of wind and we'll all be burnt to a cinder.

Jamie I didn't have a torch and the shops were shut.

Kelly It'll be OK, Cassie. It's a clear night.

Cassie It is now.

Tom You know if all the stars in the Milky Way had names and it took a second to say each one it would take one person four thousand years.

Kelly Is that so, Patrick Moore?

Cassie Shame we don't let the trees in the world hang around that long.

Kelly At least this one is going to be saved.

Tom Thanks to *toi*, and *toi* and *toi* and *moi*.

Kelly, Cassie and Tom slap each other's hands

Jamie So you reckon they'll be able to see us up here, yeah?

Cassie Aren't you supposed to be watching the rope? (*Calling*) Are you all right, Elliot? (*She goes as near to the edge as she dares*)

Tom Careful.

Cassie (*calling*) Elliot?

Elliot (*off; from behind Cassie*) Over here. I could use a bit of help getting up to join you.

They all lean over the back of the platform and pull

Elliot comes up onto the platform, holding an enormous empty margarine tub. He puts the tub down and wipes his hands on his wrists and then on his trousers

Jamie Everything lubed?

Elliot Yep, it's so well lubricated that the chain saws will slip out of their hands.

Cassie I can only hope margarine isn't detrimental to bark.

Elliot No, and it didn't contain any animal fat either. I swear.

Cassie It's just that I don't want anything to undermine this protest.

Elliot And you think I do?

Tom Lighten up, Cassie. We wouldn't have been tipped off if it weren't for Elliot.

Cassie I know. I know. I guess I'm just ... OK, positions everyone.

They all seem reluctant to move

Jamie (*to Elliot*) You're sure that they're coming tonight?

Elliot Yes, they knew the protest was planned for tomorrow and so they want to do as much as they can tonight. They're even offering to pay time and a half.

Tom Which in itself is unheard of.

Jamie Yeah. You're positive you ain't been set up?

Elliot I was listening on the extension upstairs.

Kelly And you're sure he didn't know you were listening?

Elliot Yes. He thought I was out. Then as I left to come here I overheard him trying to bribe Rachel to iron his work clothes.

Kelly What? Does he polish his hard hat an' all?

Elliot Believe me, Steve is a hat polisher of the first order.

Tom I'm convinced.

Kelly Come on then. We don't want to be caught unawares.

Cassie Ready?

They all nod and sit cross-legged on the platform. Cassie takes the sets of handcuffs and handcuffs herself to Tom on her right and Jamie on her left. She then ceremoniously throws the key away. Tom then handcuffs himself to Elliot. Elliot and Jamie go to handcuff themselves to Kelly. Each time both pairs of cuffs are locked in position the key is thrown away

Kelly Wait up. I got to do that little bit extra ... (*She stands and takes out a nail*)

Elliot Please, Kelly, don't ...

Kelly (*about the nail*) I saved it specially ...

Cassie Just sit down, can't you?

Kelly You want to make it easy for the bastards or what? (*She takes a ring out of her ear/nose/lip/mouth/belly-button and starts to nail it to the tree*)

Tom Don't do that! Please ...

Jamie D'you think it's a good idea to put it in the tree?

Kelly (*about the nail*) It won't do no harm. It's not copper. I'm allergic to that meself.

Cassie This is one of the lungs of the planet! We're all risking our lives to protect it. You'll make a travesty out of the whole thing if you damage it.

Tom Actually, iron nails can't be used in oak because the acid in the wood corrodes the iron.

Jamie But this is a sycamore tree, ain't it?

Tom I was just saying.

Kelly (*pointing to the appropriate piercing/orifice in her body*) I'm very proud of this and I'm going to use it. I am allowed to pin it to the platform, I take it ...

Cassie It's up to you ...

Kelly Ta. (*She puts the nail though the piercing in her body and nails herself to the platform*) Did you ever used to see that programme — whatsit, *Ready Steady Cook*?

Tom I don't think you've quite put us in the mood for gory yarns about food.

Kelly This ain't about food. This is about when this guy's nose stud fell into some prawn sauce stuff and Fern had to fish it out and help him put it back.

Jamie Kelly, please ...

Kelly finishes the task. With some manoeuvring Elliot and Jamie manage to cuff themselves to her

Cassie You don't worry that piercing is a form of self-mutilation?

Jamie Only for the platform.

Kelly Shouldn't we ring a few more people on the mobile to alert them?

Elliot I wish you'd suggested that before we cuffed ourselves. Let's see if I can —— (*He tries to put his hand in his pocket to get his mobile phone*)

Tom I think we should save the battery in case of emergencies. People will get wind of what's happening soon enough.

Jamie We hope.

Cassie How much support do you think there'll be tomorrow?

Jamie Don't hold your breath, this isn't horse-riding country.

Tom The road does back on to a park.

Jamie I know where it is, pal. I used to play round here when I was a kid. That's why I'm up here now.

Elliot It might back on to a park, but the people who own the houses the other side of it never go in it. They call it mugger's country.

Cassie Let's just hope these houses aren't just piles of rubble by the time they realize what's happening.

Jamie But they can't start demolishing them with us in the tree right next to them, can they?

Elliot Don't underestimate them.

Tom But we've put a few delaying tactics in place.

Elliot Yeah?

Kelly Only sugar in tank stuff.

Elliot What in what?

Tom As in refined and petrol.

Kelly Not to mention a few nails in the tyres.

Jamie And snipped cables.

Elliot What?

Tom Just H.T. leads. Rotor arms. Mainly.

Jamie Yeah, that sort of stuff.

Elliot Whose?

Cassie Those things they got lined up and parked round the back. Don't worry, we wore gloves.

Elliot Not that the thickest hard hat wouldn't be able to make an accurate guess at who did it.

Jamie Need to prove it though.

Kelly It's just machinery.

Elliot hears something

Elliot What was that?

Tom What?

Elliot Listen.

Silence

  I think I can hear someone ...

Cassie Elliot stop it.

Elliot I'm not messing about.

Kelly I can't hear anything and no one can say I haven't got my ear to the ground.

Tom   In the Arctic you know you can hear someone else's conversation from about three kilometres away.

Jamie We're not in the bloody Arctic. We're handcuffed in the dark to a tree which might be chopped down any minute and nobody will hear our screams until it's too late.

Cassie It's OK. After three. Three.

They all sing the verse which starts "We'll walk hand in hand" from the Pete Seeger song, "We Shall Overcome". Elliot looks uncomfortable and Jamie is very embarrassed

Jamie It's bad enough without having to sing this embarrassing old hippie shit.

Cassie It serves two purposes. While keeping our spirits up, it will alert them to our presence.

Jamie Yeah? Well, it's doing my head in.

Tom I didn't hear anything anyway ...

Elliot Shush.

Kelly You know I think I can hear something ...

Cassie The position you're in, I'm surprised you can even breathe, never mind hear.

Jamie Probably you only heard a bird or something scratching underneath the platform ...

Elliot I heard footsteps.

Tom (*shouting*) Anyone there?

Silence

Cassie (*singing*) "We are not afraid ..."

Elliot suddenly manages to slide his hands out of his cuffs, climbs from the platform and disappears from view

What are you doing?

Tom Elliot ... ?
Kelly He's freaked.

There is a loud crack. It could be the sound of a branch snapping, a gun firing or a car back-firing

Cassie What was that?
Tom Sounded like a branch snapping.
Jamie (*shouting*) You all right? Elliot?
Kelly He must have slipped ...
Jamie Sounded more like a gun shot to me.
Cassie Jamie, please! Where's the mobile ...
Kelly He had it. Elliot. (*Shouting*) Elliot.
Tom It could have just been a car back-firing ...
Cassie Move towards the edge. Let's see if we can see him.

Still handcuffed, obviously, they all shuffle as best they can towards the edge. Jamie is the one who has to lean over

All Elliot!

Silence

Jamie I can't see anything. He must have legged it.
Cassie He's not answering us. State the obvious, Cassie.
Jamie He wouldn't, would he? If he'd bottled out.
Kelly Suppose he's hurt?
Cassie Are you sure you can see?
Tom If we all slowly move up, we can lower Jamie over the edge so he can have a better look.
Jamie It's OK. I can see. I can see. And I can't see any broken branches or him. I'm telling you, he's gone.

SCENE 4

Underneath the tree platform

Elliot and Lucy have fallen on top of one another. Lucy is from 1913. She has a toffee hammer

They disentangle themselves. Lucy, frightened, tries to fight Elliot off, and drops her toffee hammer in the process

Lucy Get away from me, you disgusting oaf.

Elliot I don't want to be anywhere near you.

Lucy Likewise.

Elliot And what do you think you're doing?

Lucy What do you mean, what am I doing? I'm trying to get you off me.

Elliot I don't want to be on you. I think I must have slipped. I'm sorry. (*He stands up and backs away from her*)

Lucy Who are you?

Elliot What's it to you? (*Beat*) My name's Elliot if you must know. And yours?

Lucy Lucy.

Elliot Are you all right, Lucy?

Lucy I'll have to be won't I? And you?

Elliot I think so. Were you coming to join the protest?

Lucy And what business is it of yours, if I was?

Elliot There's no need to look so worried. I'm part of it. Was.

Lucy You? (*She starts looking on the ground for her hammer*) Or has he sent you to spy on me?

Elliot Who? You dropped something?

Lucy Yes. It was in my hand. It's got to be here somewhere.

Elliot No one sent me to spy ...

Lucy In my experience, if you don't mind me saying, it's very unusual to find men in the protest.

Elliot Then you can't have much experience, if you don't mind me saying, because it's not like Greenham. There's a lot of men now.

Lucy I don't mean to be rude but you're not making much sense. Are you sure your brains didn't take a scrambling?

Elliot Don't take it the wrong way, of course we owe a lot to women. It's still very female, the way we protest — nurturing, peaceful, respectful of Mother Earth ...

Lucy That's ridiculously old-fashioned. Where have you been? We're not simpery Madonnas any more.

Elliot Funny, I never thought of Madonna as simpery — but then I was a bit too young to be into her ...

Lucy We're more at home with a bomb than a bottle. Nurture ho. You are behind the times. We smash things now. (*Finding and holding aloft her toffee hammer*) That's what these are for. Deeds not words.

Elliot I agree with direct action but it doesn't have to be violent. In fact it's important that it's never violent.

Lucy Then you can't care much about the cause. Emily is still seriously ill in hospital.

Elliot Who's she?

Lucy Don't you read the papers? Her what run out in front of His Majesty's horse.

Elliot I hope the horse wasn't hurt.

Lucy No, but she's not yet regained consciousness.

Elliot I don't agree with some of the methods of hunt saboteurs.

Lucy It was a horse race!

Elliot Like, as in Epsom Park?

Lucy That's exactly where it was! You was having me on, wasn't you? Just now. You know all about it. (*She feels faint*) Ooh, I don't know what's happened to me.

Elliot I think you've fallen.

Lucy Are you a doctor now or what?

Elliot No.

Lucy Then don't say that. Please. Please don't let that be true.

Elliot It looks like you're OK though.

Lucy Like I'm what? What's that?

Elliot It's all right. I'll stay here with you. Make sure you're all right.

Lucy (*pinching herself*) I told him I had a gentleman friend looking out for me. Now, looks like I dreamt one up.

Elliot Let's just sit down for a bit and get our breath back.

Lucy Don't you start nothing.

Elliot Of course not.

Lucy No, of course you can't. If you're in my imagination, you'll do anything I want.

Elliot I don't know what you're on but I don't think you should be taking a trip like that, not on your own.

Scene 5

The tree platform. Night

Kelly, Cassie, Tom and Jamie are handcuffed together up the tree. They are beginning to feel cold, tired and hungry

Kelly I reckon it was my piercing what sent him over the edge.

Cassie Don't blame yourself.

Tom No, we shouldn't have mentioned destroying the equipment. He doesn't agree with that.

Cassie I know. He's a fully paid up, dyed-in-the-wool fluffy.

Jamie I don't reckon it was nothing to do with that. I reckon he knew he was going to bottle it before he sat down.

Kelly Is that right, Miss Marple?

Jamie Did you see when he'd finished greasing the tree, he wiped his hands on his wrists? Believe me, he was leaving his options open right from the off.

Kelly I'm beginning to wish I'd done the same. At least not nailed myself down.

Cassie Bit Christian, the symbolism, isn't it?

Jamie I don't like to say nothing but I think it's barbaric.

Tom As I recall Christ wasn't crucified through the ear.

Kelly Can someone try and help me with this?

Tom Not with my eyes open. It makes me too queasy.

Jamie Me too.

Kelly You're as gutless as Elliot you are ——

Jamie Either that or he was a plant.

Tom A what?

Jamie Think about it. He could be working for them, like his brother.

Cassie But if he was, he wouldn't admit that his brother was, would he?

Tom I suppose it could be a double bluff.

Cassie Can we stop talking about him and do something else?

Tom Being handcuffed together hardly lends itself to a game of Scrabble.

Jamie Yeah, whose stupid idea was that?

Cassie See that? On the side of the house.

Kelly No, actually. I can't move my head in case you hadn't noticed.

Tom All it is, is a tiny window which has been bricked up.

Jamie So? The house was converted into flats.

Cassie Yes, in the eighties. But that window was blocked up years ago. You've only got to look at the discolouration of the bricks.

Tom And?

Cassie So why would you brick up a window?

Kelly Window tax?

Tom The house isn't that old. The window tax was in the eighteenth century. These were only built at the turn of the century.

Kelly If I'd wanted to be on "University Challenge", I'd have gone to university.

Cassie All right, point taken.

Jamie Go on — why was it blocked up?

Cassie Apparently the daughter of the house had a boyfriend who used to climb up this tree and talk to her through the bedroom window but her father got to know about it. So one night the father goes out with a gun and lies in wait at the bottom of this very tree for the young man. He dozes off but sure enough, just past midnight he sees a figure up in the branches. It must have been that branch there. The father pulls the trigger and the figure falls and lies motionless at his feet. He then discovers that he's shot his beloved daughter who, unbeknownst to him, had planned to elope that very evening with her lover by climbing out of her bedroom window and down the tree. He then ordered that the window be bricked up.

Kelly How could they be lovers if she just talked to him through the window?

Cassie You know what I mean. They were obviously in love and he taught her how to climb out of her window and she was to meet him and run off ...

Tom Each man kills the thing he loves the most ...

Jamie Do what?

Tom Oscar Wilde ...

Kelly Oh bloody hell.

Jamie How come he mistook his daughter for a bloke?

Cassie It was dark.

Jamie Even so.

Cassie Short-sighted?

Tom When someone starts to lose their sight, the brain lacks stimulus and it can make up images, like hallucinations ...

Kelly Is that so, Dr Raj Persaud?

Cassie It's just a myth.

Jamie How come you knew it?

Cassie When I was trying to find out more about this place from the local history library ...

Kelly You went in a tree tomb. You traitor.

Cassie Pardon?

Kelly What were the books made out of? Or were they the product of recycled lungs or what?

In the distance there is a flashing orange light. The others become aware of it. Silence

I was only joking. No offence.

Tom Shush.

Kelly Don't you start ... (*She sees the orange light; realizing*) This isn't an hallucination, is it?

Cassie If it is, it's a collective one.

Jamie Here we go, here we go ...

The light gets brighter. There is the noise of engines. The noise grows louder as the vehicles get closer. There is the sound of men tramping through the park, and of chainsaws being started

Underneath the tree platform

Elliot and Lucy are as they were by the tree. Elliot is looking at the inscription on the hammer

Elliot And the S?

Lucy Guess who gave it to me?

Elliot I can't.

Lucy Guess.

Elliot I don't know anyone you know.

Lucy You might not know her personally but you'll have heard of her.

Elliot Scary Spice?

Lucy Sylvia.

Elliot (*not understanding*) Oh Sylvia. Right.

Lucy Anyway. (*She takes the hammer*) It's been very pleasant talking to you, but I must remind you I'm on a mission.

Elliot Right you are, Scully.

Lucy Do you mind? I am the chamber maid. I have nothing to do with the scullery.

Elliot Sounds kinky. How about I come with you and then how about we go for a burger?

Lucy For who? You're sure he hasn't sent you?

Elliot Who?

Lucy Master George.

Elliot No, I told you. Where are you going now with that little hammer?

Lucy None of your business.

Elliot You go then. I'll wait here for you to come back.

Lucy I'm not coming back here.

Elliot I thought you said you worked here.

Lucy I have decided to terminate my employment forthwith.

Elliot What will you do?

Lucy I have ambitions. Well, dreams ...

Elliot Yeah and you think I'm one.

Lucy And a very amicable one you've proved to be. You know I've never told a living soul this but what I want more than anything is to go to university.

Elliot Why haven't you told anyone?

Lucy Because they'd laugh at me.

Elliot Why should they?

Lucy Well, me ...

Elliot I know it's expensive but you could take out a loan.

Lucy I could study but they still wouldn't let me get a degree ...

Elliot Why not?

Lucy Because I'm a woman.

Elliot (*laughing*) That's ridiculous.

Lucy Why, do you think I'm a man?

Elliot Of course you can go. Women can do anything now. That's the time we live in.

Lucy It's so easy for you to say.

Elliot This victim mentality isn't doing you any good.

Lucy I'm not quite sure what you mean but I'm quite sure I can't wait for further explanation. I'll keep you no longer.

Elliot Hang on just a bit. I don't feel well.

Lucy What is it?

Elliot My head hurts something chronic.

Lucy Shall I see if I can go and get help?

Elliot No, no. I'll be all right in a couple of minutes.

Scene 7

The tree platform. Night

The tree top is lit from below. There is the sense that there are a great many people underneath the tree. There is the sound of chainsaws, etc.

Cassie, Kelly, Jamie and Tom are as they were, handcuffed together

Cassie We've just got to keep calm and let them know we're here.

Kelly That might not make us any safer.

Jamie They've got chainsaws.

Tom I don't think any police have arrived. They'll be able to do what they like. It'll be our word against theirs.

They sing "We Shall Not Be Moved"

The noise from below stops but they are interrupted by a man using a loud hailer

Man (*off; through a loud hailer*) Oi! One of your lot is down here, hurt.

Cassie Elliot?

Jamie Take no notice. It's a trick.

Tom I thought you said you were sure he'd gone.

Jamie I was. I am.

Man (*off; through a loud hailer*) He looks in a bad way. We'll need your help to know what happened.

Cassie They're bluffing.

Jamie How can you be so sure?

Cassie Elliot said his brother was working for them. If his brother is down there, his brother would say, "Hey, this is my brother. His name is Elliot, etc., etc.," Wouldn't he? (*Shouting down*) What's his name?

Man (*off; through a loud hailer*) He's not got I.D. on him.

They look at each other

Jamie Cassie's got a point.

Man (*off; through a loud hailer*) For fuck's sake, what's more important, him or the tree?

Tom What should we do?

Kelly What can we do?

Man (*off; through a loud hailer*) We've got people down here coming up, but it would be better if you came down ...

Kelly It sounds like a ruse ...

Cassie Call their bluff ...

There is the sound of ambulance sirens

Tom What bluff? Even they wouldn't risk dialling 999 as a hoax.
Cassie (*to Jamie*) I thought you said you definitely saw him run off.
Jamie I said I'd thought he'd run off. I couldn't see him.
Kelly You don't know the ambulance is coming here.
Cassie Maybe they've called in advance of cutting the tree down with us in it.
Tom You know what ——
Kelly No, and what's more we don't want to. I vote we give ourselves up.
Cassie You don't know that Elliot is down there.
Tom But I'm not going to take that chance.
Jamie Me neither. (*Calling down*) We're locked on up here but we're prepared to give up.
Kelly Please someone help me get the nail out before they get to us.
Cassie Elliot, you've ruined the whole thing. Because of you, this tree will die. I just hope you can live with that.

SCENE 8

A living-room

Alana is alone

Gemma comes in wearing the toffee hammer from a key ring on her belt

Alana Where have you been?
Gemma Grandma's.
Alana Where did you get that?
Gemma It was in that tin of Great-Grandma's stuff.
Alana Let's have a look.

Gemma takes the toffee hammer off and hands it to Alana

Gemma It's got some engraving on the back.

Alana What's it say?

Gemma Nothing. It doesn't make sense.

Alana F.L.Y.I.T.C.S.

Gemma What do you reckon it means?

Alana F.L.Y — Fly. I.T.C.S. Information Training Centres. Information Training Centres for Flies?

Gemma (*about the hammer*) You can have it if you want.

Alana Na, I'm too old for this sort of thing. (*Beat*) You're being a bit nice all of a sudden. What do you want?

Gemma I'm stuck with my course work.

Alana I thought you'd just come back from interviewing Nanna.

Gemma I have.

Alana And?

Gemma Apart from saying that it was actually rather oppressive to have your mother alive for most of your life.

Alana Not nearly as oppressive as having your little sister alive all your life ——

Gemma You better get yourself a job so you can save up for a contract killer 'cos if nature takes its course you'll be dead before me.

Alana Oh happy day.

Gemma Don't say that. Don't even joke about it.

Alana What's it to you? You know they want to switch the machine off for that tree boy.

Gemma It's like they said, don't dwell on it.

Alana They haven't though, only because they still haven't been able to get hold of his mum.

Gemma I wish our parents would go on holiday without us.

Alana Not much chance of that now. Go on say it. Thanks to me.

Gemma I wasn't going to say that. Grandma asked after you.

Alana What did she say, how oppressive it was knowing I was still alive?

Gemma No, she said she wants to see you ——

Alana Did she? Did she tell you how Great Nanna went from being in service to university?

Gemma No, that's just it, she wouldn't.

Alana Oh my God, it must be something loathsome and odious.

Gemma Will you go and see her —— ?

Alana No way.

Gemma But she said she'd tell you.

Alana You mean I'm so low, I can't be corrupted any further.

Gemma Go on.

Alana She didn't ask to see me, did she?

Gemma Yes, she did and she said she'll only tell you.

Alana You've just made that up so I'll go round there. She was glad I didn't go to the funeral because I'd show everyone up. Her mother was so — whatever she was ... Nanna can't even bring herself to tell you. Ha. It looks like it's genetic. I come from a long line of no-good-waste-of-space-fuck-up-losers.

SCENE 9

The special care room in hospital

Rachel is sitting by Elliot's bed. Elliot is lifeless

Rachel Elliot, I could kill you. Just come back, wake up. Mum is on her way home ——

Steve comes in

Steve She's arriving at Heathrow this evening.

Rachel What time?

Steve She doesn't want us to meet her. She wants us to stay here and talk to Elliot.

Rachel What did you tell her?

Steve Only that he'd had a fall and was in a coma. Don't worry, I didn't mention they were waiting for her advice before they switched off the machine.

Rachel He probably wouldn't be in this state if someone had called the ambulance sooner but I don't suppose you mentioned that either.

Steve How many more times? Hundreds of us were told to go to that site. It was like a military operation or something. We were told to advance in rows and not to break the line and get on with the job of demolishing the houses. I had no idea he was there.

Rachel Someone must have called an ambulance.

Steve We knew they'd found a body.

Rachel And you're telling me, it never crossed your mind that it could have been Elliot?

Steve I didn't think.

Rachel Come on. You must have seen the ambulance arrive ...

Steve Yeah.

Rachel And you must have seen who went in it. And recognized him.

Steve I didn't get close enough.

Rachel Have you apologized to him?

Steve For what? I haven't done anything.

Rachel Except wind him up by getting a job as one of those pathetic bailiff's lackeys.

Steve He wound me up more like by getting involved in those daft tree-top protests. You seem to have conveniently forgotten that you also used to go into one when he started spouting that pretentious eco-warrior, Earth-firster jargon.

Rachel At least his choice was one of principle.

Steve Oh yes, principle. That luxury afforded to the privileged few. He can take a year out of his studies. He has a place at university. They'll wait. Someone like him, they'll hold their breath. He's worth waiting for. People with principles never have to take jobs that pay three forty an hour. They're allowed principles but I'm not supposed to be allowed the dignity of taking the only job that I've been offered in a year. If I had a choice maybe then I'd have principles.

Rachel Everyone has choice.

Steve Where d'you get that idea? Off *Songs of Praise*?

Rachel We shouldn't be doing this, not with his friends waiting outside. I'm sorry.

Steve Me too. No, I am.

Rachel moves to speak to Kelly who is off stage

Rachel You can come in, now.

Kelly tentatively approaches. She has an enormous Elastoplast over her nose or ear, whichever place has had the nail removed from it

Kelly Thanks ... . I'm not sure ...
Rachel We'll wait over here ...

Rachel and Steve stand back from the others

Kelly Elliot ... Hi. They've said we should come and say goodbye ... I wanted to show you the nail. It's still got a bit of my nose hanging on it — look. I thought it would make you laugh — or gag or something ... Actually, I thought it might shock you enough to make you open your eyes — I really wish I had the power to do that.

Jamie comes in and goes over to Elliot

Jamie Pal, you got to buck up or they are going to pull the plug. I really couldn't see you lying down the bottom there, you know that, don't you? (*Beat*) But also I was frightened, wasn't I, to lean over further ... If I had — maybe I would have seen you ... But I suddenly freaked being tied up there and was terrified I'd slip over, dragging the others on top of me. Please, mate, just come round, if only to tell me it's all right.

Tom comes in and goes over to Elliot

Tom Elliot, you know that the human nervous system has a greater number of possible connections than a telephone exchange with a line to every person on earth. Mate, you just need to connect and pick up the receiver.

Cassie comes in and goes over to Elliot

Cassie I think it's important that you know that because you're lying here, they don't dare cut down the tree. We don't even have to maintain a presence there. You can't get near it in fact for the flowers that surround it. And everyday there's been more. You're a national hero, Elliot. You and you alone saved it. Thank you.

Rachel sees Jamie, Cassie and Tom out. As they exit, they smile appropriately at Rachel but give Steve dirty looks. Rachel exits after them

When Steve is alone he goes over to Elliot

Steve All right, I have always been jealous of you and her come to that, but I didn't do it out of spite or jealousy. I did know it was you lying there and I pretended I didn't know you. They've located Mum, your mum, and she's on her way back. It would be brilliant if you weren't lying here now because, mate, I'm having a hard time of it here. It's hard to admit, it's just that some of those guys, the muppets with the chainsaws, they make Reservoir Dogs look like an advert for Pedigree Chum. I didn't want it to be you but I was afraid, in front of the others, to own up to knowing you. And scared that the bosses would think I'd tipped you lot off. I was ashamed, humiliated, I stood there doing nothing and feeling sick but it's nothing to how bad I feel now. Your mother's on her way back. Please, Elliot don't let me have to face her without you.

SCENE 10

Underneath the tree platform

Elliot and Lucy are as they were underneath the tree

Elliot My head feels loads better ... I think I can sleep now. You go ...
Lucy Come on, get up, go back to your friends ...
Elliot I can't face them. I've been too much of a coward.
Lucy You can't sleep here ...
Elliot I'm so tired I could sleep anywhere ...
Lucy It's too cold ...
Elliot (*very drowsy*) It's not. I'll be fine.

Lucy hears something

Lucy What was that?
Elliot What?
Lucy Someone's watching us.
Elliot (*mumbling*) You're imagining it.
Lucy (*shaking Elliot*) It's him! It's him!
Elliot (*unable to rouse himself*) There's no-one there.
Lucy There is — look. I'm for it now.
Elliot Take a deep breath.
Lucy So will you be ... Please go ... Just go ...
Elliot (*trying to rouse himself*) I can't. I can't see anyone.
Lucy Elliot, run ... Get away ... Get help ...

Elliot with great effort rouses himself but is unable to see Lucy

Elliot Lucy? What's happening? Where are you?

SCENE 11

The special care room in hospital

Steve sits at Elliot's hospital bedside. Elliot twitches

Steve Do that again? And again? Elliot, speak to me. Can you? Elliot? (*He moves towards the door; calling*) Nurse?
Elliot Lucy?
Steve What? Did you say something?
Elliot Lucy.
Steve It's me, Steve ...
Elliot Lucy.
Steve Who are you pissing well calling Lucy? Stop winding me up.
Elliot (*becoming distressed; calling out*) Where is she? What's happened to her?
Steve It's all right it's me — Steve. You're safe.
Elliot (*shouting*) Lucy?
Steve Hold on mate. I'm going to get someone. Just hold on.

SCENE 12

The living-room

Gemma sits alone

Alana bursts in

Alana Lucy was Great-Nanna's name, wasn't it?

Gemma So?

Alana If I go round to see Nanna and get the info, will you come to the hospital with me?

Gemma The hospital? Alana? You're not?

Alana Of course not. How could I be? I haven't been out for weeks. No, you know they were waiting for that bloke's mother to get back from holiday ...

Gemma What?

Alana Before they could switch the life-support machine off. The tree-top one. Elliot. He's come round. But he's gone Harpic. He keeps calling for someone called Lucy.

Gemma How could that possibly have anything to do with Great-Grandma?

Alana I don't know, do I, but they're asking for anyone called Lucy who knows him to come forward to jog his memory.

Gemma That'll be hard, or were you planning to take a medium with you?

Alana Don't be sick. It might get me in to see him ——

Gemma Do you really think that's such a good idea?

Alana I don't know.

Gemma Then ...

Alana Don't you think it's worth a try?

Gemma Don't ask me.

Alana If I could help him somehow I wouldn't feel so shit about ——

Gemma OK. Deal.

SCENE 13

The special care room in hospital

*Elliot is sitting up in bed. Jamie, Kelly, Cassie and Tom are visiting.
Steve stands watching some way off*

Kelly I used to know a Lucy.

Elliot Yeah?

Kelly But I don't think you ever met her. She was a dinner lady at
my primary school.

Cassie Kelly!

Kelly At least I'm trying.

Elliot She was at the bottom of the tree.

Cassie So you keep saying.

Jamie She couldn't have been, pal. I'd have seen her.

Elliot You remember we heard footsteps?

Jamie I don't think I heard nothing until they all came swarming
through the park.

Elliot Before. When we were on the platform. You heard them too,
Kelly.

Kelly I can't say I did really. Having my ear squashed against the
platform was a bit like having it against a shell. Sounds got
distorted.

Tom You were unconscious, Elliot. If there had been someone with
you when they found you, they'd have seen her as well.

Elliot Yeah, they took her. They took her somewhere. She didn't
want to go.

*The others look at each other and Jamie starts to hum the X-Files
theme music*

Cassie Shut up, Jamie. Haven't you ever heard of post-traumatic
stress disorder? I think we should go and let Elliot get some rest.

*Alana and Gemma come in and go up to Steve. The others go
leaving Elliot alone*

Alana We're here to visit Elliot.

Steve (*looking at her suspiciously*) And you are?

Alana Er ... Lucy.

Steve (*recognizing her*) And the rest. What do you think my name is, Jack Arse, Jack Shit? I read the papers you know. Just get lost before I get you thrown out of here.

Alana I've come to see Elliot.

Steve He's getting all the drugs he needs.

Gemma Hang on ——

Steve I don't know who you are but I know who she is. She was in the papers for selling "E" to that lad what dropped dead and she's just been excluded from school. You should be locked up, not allowed to roam around hospitals. How dare you turn up here?

Alana I think I might be able to help him.

Steve What is your problem? Not been in the limelight for a couple of weeks, is that it? You want me to call the police? You a publicity junkie or what?

Gemma She risked coming here to see if she could help your brother. If he was my brother I think I'd try it, wouldn't you?

Steve And you are?

Gemma Her sister.

Steve Her real sister?

Alana Unfortunately.

Gemma and Steve both look at Alana

For her.

Steve How come you talk so different?

Alana She won a scholarship to a private school.

Gemma A snob school. Now are you going to let us talk to your brother or what?

Steve Whatever it is you got to say you can say it to me.

Alana All right, I know it might sound weird but ——

Gemma Don't tell him. If he won't let you see Elliot we'll go. Come on.

Steve Wait up. You can see him but I'll be sitting in. And I want you gone by the time my mother and sister get here.

They all move up to Elliot

Alana Hi.

Elliot (*warily*) Hallo.

Alana I've come to talk to you about Lucy ...

Elliot You're not her.

Alana No, but ——

Elliot You do look a bit similar.

Alana I hope not. She was a hundred and one and totally Harpic.

Elliot looks puzzled

Gemma (*by way of explanation*) Clean round the bend.

Alana On top of which she's been buried a week.

Elliot Not the same one then. She was only about your age.

Alana This is all going to sound completely mad, right. She was in service in that house. You know what that means?

Elliot She was a maid who had to live in ...

Alana Yeah. Anyway, she was a bit of a slapper by all accounts an' all.

Elliot Really.

Gemma She doesn't mean that.

Alana That's what Nanna told me.

Gemma Our great-grandmother's daughter.

Elliot She said that about her own mother?

Alana That's what she meant. Apparently she was used to entertaining men in her bedroom. One night the son of the house thought he heard someone breaking in and he went out and thinking he saw a burglar up the tree, he shot him. Only it was dark and it wasn't a bloke but our great-grandmother, Lucy, obviously Luce by name loose by nature, who had been climbing out to meet her lover.

Elliot But I thought you said that she only died last week?

Alana Because she wasn't shot dead. She survived. The family didn't want any trouble from the police so they gave her wads of money to be quiet.

Elliot Slapper is a rather sexually derogatory word to use about your own mother.

Gemma I think it's weird that she told her daughter about it.

Alana No, she didn't tell Nanna anything. But they moved back into this area when Nanna was a little girl, and she heard people talking about it. Lucy never talked about her time in service until the end of her life when it was like she didn't know whether she was talking out loud or not.

Elliot It's all so strange — it's like a dream now. She was a bit stunned and when I said I thought she must have fallen, she looked panic-stricken.

Alana She'd just fallen out of a tree from a great height after being shot. She'd have to be some cool babe to be serene about it.

Elliot No, I think the son of the house was sexually harassing her. That's what it was — I think she was worried she might even be pregnant ...

Gemma She told you all that?

Elliot I don't suppose she was as inhibited as she might have been if she'd thought me real. She believed that she'd dreamt me up. To get him off her back.

Alana Off her front don't you mean?

Elliot Don't you see, she threatened him with a boyfriend. He must have been scared that the bloke would come and beat him up or something so he went out with the intention of shooting him and if caught he was going to say that he thought the boyfriend was a burglar. However, he shot her by mistake.

Gemma Then how come everyone thought she was a woman of very loose morals?

Elliot That was probably part of the deal with the family to protect their son. They'd give her money as long as she stuck to their version of the story. And once she'd taken the money and given her word she never went back on it.

Alana She sold out.

Elliot Did she go to university?

Gemma Yes.

Elliot Well, that's what she did with the money.

Silence

Gemma Amazing.

Alana What a shame Gran and Mum never knew. They could have
   been proud of her.

Elliot sees the hammer hanging from Gemma's belt

Elliot That's her hammer.

Gemma (*she takes it off her belt and shows it to Elliot*) It was, yeah.

Elliot Yes. Look. F.L.Y.I.T.C.S. Did she tell you what that stood
   for?

Gemma No. I only got this after she died.

Elliot For — Lucy — Yours — In — The — Cause — Sylvia.

Gemma No kidding. What, Sylvia, as in Pankhurst?

Elliot That's why she was so proud of it.

Silence

Alana So when you get out of here, you want to go for a burger
   sometime or what?

Elliot I'm afraid I'm a veggie.

Alana That's like "Sorry, I'm washing my hair!", right?

Elliot Thanks though ...

Alana Actually, it's her you have to thank. She did all the work.

Gemma No, I never.

Alana (*shrugging*) I think I'll go for a Coke. (*Calling over her
   shoulder to Steve*) Black liquid as opposed to white powder. (*To
   Gemma*) Meet you back at the canteen.

Steve follows Alana

Steve Thanks. Hey, hold up. I just wanted to say thanks. I really do
   appreciate it.

Alana Yeah, right.

Steve Sorry he gave you the brush off.

Alana I don't mean to be offensive but I'd sort of gone off him the
   minute he opened his gob.

Steve Oh, yeah?

Alana Listen, if there's one thing I can't stand it's boys who slap you down by politically correcting your fucking language.

Steve What can you stand then?

Alana Don't waste your breath asking.

Steve I know this much. You like shocking people.

Alana Everyone's supposed to be good at something, aren't they?

Alana goes

Scene 14

Underneath the tree platform

The foot of the tree is surrounded by floral tributes. Elliot and Gemma stand looking at the tributes

Elliot This is too weird. It's like I've died.

Gemma I suppose you nearly did.

Elliot Yeah and in 1913 so did your great-grandmother.

Gemma If she had then she wouldn't have been my great-grandmother, if you see what I mean, and Grandma wouldn't have been born then neither would my mother or I ——

Elliot Stop it. You're doing my head in. Why wouldn't your gran tell you the story about her?

Gemma At first I thought it was because it involved sex but I don't think it was that actually. I think she thought it would help Alana.

Elliot How?

Gemma (*shrugging*) Explaining that her great-grandmother survived a great trauma but was able to get on and make something of her life?

Elliot And has it had any effect?

Gemma Yeah, it seems to have worked. She spends less time in front of the TV and she's been a lot nicer to me.

Elliot That must be a relief.

Gemma Feels very strange. Not as strange as you having met my great-grandmother when she was only a girl. How do you explain that?

Elliot I don't know ...

Gemma If I wrote any of this down, they'd probably send me to see the Ed. Psych. To have my head examined.

Elliot (*holding her head*) Ah, yes very unusual, descended from a matriarchal line of headstrong, intellectual and attractive women. (*He leans over to kiss her*)

Gemma turns away

Sorry — sorry ...

Gemma I just had a horrible thought — that I might turn into a hundred-and-one-year-old woman ... Did you kiss her?

Elliot No!

Gemma Oh, well, I guess that makes — it a bit better ... But I also get the feeling that someone's watching us.

Elliot Not again. Keep still. (*He looks around*) Oh yes. Over there.

Gemma What's he doing here?

Elliot I think he's following me ...

Gemma Creepy.

Elliot Ever since I got well he's been very protective. It was much better when he wanted to kill me.

Gemma Do you think he's seen us?

Elliot Let's see if we can give him the slip. Come on.

SCENE 15

The tree platform

Alana stands alone

Steve climbs up

Alana (*jumping*) What are you doing here?

Steve Spying on my step-brother.

Alana They've gone.

Steve Do you do the same then?

Alana The same what?

Steve Making sure she's OK. Ever since it happened, I want to make sure Elliot's OK.

Alana Gemma will always be OK. No, I thought I'd come here to see if I could feel what my great-grandmother felt when she fell out of this thing. I didn't realize Gemma had a date with Elliot.

Steve You jealous?

Alana shakes her head

I am.

Alana You're too bloody old for my sister.

Steve No, no. I mean of him. His belief in something, that it matters, that he's prepared to put his life on hold for it, that he has friends who feel the same. Oh, shit, I feel embarrassed now.

Alana It's easy to believe in something. Why don't we start the "Give concrete and exhaust pipes a break" movement?

Steve (*laughing*) Yeah, you know the worst thing about all this environmental mania is that it will push up the price of cars and I can't ever see myself affording one as it is.

Alana Still, I suppose it's thanks to them that this park's still here. Imagine if poor people had nowhere to go but walk round and round the locked shopping centre of an evening, watching others stuffing their faces in restaurants where you can buy champagne by the glass and being able to spend more money on "Pick and Mix" sweets in the cinema than on the film.

Steve Are your parents hard up, then?

Alana Take no notice. I'm talking out of my arse.

Steve Do they know where you are?

Alana No.

Steve Will they be worried?

Alana If they find I'm not in my room, yeah. But making me stay in is, I think, more about their concern about someone beating me up than wanting to punish me.

Steve (*taking some money from his pocket*) You don't fancy ...

Alana What are you doing, trying to give me money for sex?

Steve No!

Alana I will if you want.

Steve I was going to say I've got money for a film and some "Pick and Mix".

Alana No, thanks, I want to stay here, but you go ahead.

Steve I thought you knew how your great-grandmother fell.

Alana Suppose she didn't fall though? Suppose she jumped? Suppose she was pregnant and so ashamed she couldn't face it so she threw herself out of the window?

Steve Suppose she did, so what? (*Beat*) No, don't even think about it. You don't have to do the same. Things are different these days.

Alana How?

Steve There are abortions for starters.

Alana I'm not pregnant. That would be easy — so much easier.

Steve Than what?

Alana Being me. Being the girl that sold the "E" that killed him. Whatever I do I will always be known as that girl and even if I'm not I'll always know it. There'll be days and days like this and months and years. But if I jumped out of this tree do you think I might be able to meet him and tell him not to take it and that he would then live until he was a hundred and one?

Steve No, I think that's barking.

Alana What, as in, up the wrong tree?

Steve Yeah.

Alana shrugs and turns away

You have to move forward.

Alana I don't know how.

Steve What do you want?

Alana I want to be brave enough to jump.

Steve Sometimes the most courageous thing to do is keep breathing.

THE END

FURNITURE AND PROPERTY LIST

On stage: Television
                Remote Control

Off stage: Old biscuit tin (**Gemma**)

SCENE 2

On stage: Hospital bed
                Two chairs

SCENE 3

On stage: Tree with platform
                Torch for **Cassie**
                Rope for **Tom**
                Five sets of handcuffs

Off stage: Enormous, empty margarine tub (**Elliot**)

Personal: **Kelly**: ear-ring or other piercing, nail

SCENE 4

On stage: Tree as SCENE 3
                Toffee hammer with inscription for **Lucy**

SCENE 5

On stage: Tree as SCENE 3
                No additional props

Scene 6

On stage: As Scene 4

Scene 7

On stage: As Scene 3

Scene 8

On stage: As Scene 1

Off stage: Toffee hammer for **Gemma**

Scene 9

On stage: As Scene 2

Personal: **Kelly**: Large elastoplast

Scene 10

On stage: As Scene 4

Scene 11

On stage: As Scene 2

Scene 12

On stage: As Scene 1

Scene 13

On stage: As Scene 2

Scene 14

On stage: As Scene 4
                Floral tributes

Scene 15

On stage: Tree platform as Scene 2

Personal: **Steve**: money

LIGHTING PLOT

Practical fittings required: television flicker effect

Scene 1

To open: General interior lighting; television flicker effect on

No cues

Scene 2

To open: Hospital interior lighting

No cues

Scene 3

To open: Exterior lighting; night

Cue 1	**Cassie** switches on her torch *Covering spot on torch*	(Page 5)

Scene 4

To open: General exterior lighting

No cues

Scene 5

To open: Exterior lighting; night

Cue 2	**Kelly**: " ... recycled lungs or what?" *Flashing orange light*	(Page 26)

Cue 3   **Jamie**: " ... here we go."   (Page 16)
            Brighten orange flashing light

SCENE 6

To open: General exterior lighting

No cues

SCENE 7

To open: Exterior lighting; night. Tree top is lit from below

No cues

SCENE 8

To open: General interior lighting

No cues

SCENE 9

To open: Hospital interior lighting

No cues

SCENE 10

To open: General exterior lighting

No cues

SCENE 11

To open: Hospital interior lighting

No cues

SCENE 12

To open: General interior lighting

No cues

SCENE 13

To open: Hospital interior lighting

No cues

SCENE 14

To open: General exterior lighting

No cues

SCENE 15

To open: General interior lighting

No cues

EFFECTS PLOT

Cue 1	**Kelly**: " He's freaked."	(Page 11)
	Loud crack like a branch snap, gun fire or car back-fire	
Cue 2	**Jamie**: " ... here we go..."	(Page 16)
	Sound of engines growing louder as the vehicles get closer. Sound of men trampling through the park and chainsaws being started up	
Cue 3	To open SCENE 7	(Page 18)
	Sound of a lot of people and chainsaws	
Cue 4	**Cassie, Kelly, Jamie** and **Tom** sing	(Page 19)
	Cut chainsaw and quieten crowd noise. Man uses loud hailer dialogue as p19	
Cue 5	**Cassie**: "Call their bluff ..."	(Page 19)
	Ambulance sirens